SIGNS *from the* UNIVERSE

A Journal for Interpreting Symbols & Finding Meaning in Everyday Magic

Nadia Hayes

CASTLE POINT BOOKS
NEW YORK

ISBN 978-1-250-28517-1 (trade paperback)

Design by Melissa Gerber
Edited by Aimee Chase
Images used under license from Shutterstock.com

Our books may be purchased in bulk for promotional, educational,
or business use. Please contact your local bookseller or the Macmillan
Corporate and Premium Sales Department at 1-800-221-7945, extension 5442,
or by email at MacmillanSpecialMarkets@macmillan.com.

First Edition: 2023

10 9 8 7 6 5 4 3 2 1

This
JOURNAL
belongs to:

_____

INTRODUCTION

Let the Universe be your trusted guide

YOU ARE AN ESSENTIAL PART OF THE WONDROUS FABRIC OF THIS GREAT UNIVERSE. Its ancient language is written deep within you—all you have to do is trust that you already know it. Once you begin to take notice of, and heed, the Universe's artful array of signs and symbols, you can head more confidently in the direction of your dreams.

Let *Signs from the Universe* be a daily bridge to the wisdom of the spiritual world, a trusty companion to help you decode the magical, transformative messages that seem to materialize when you need them most. Whether it's a dream of flying, a butterfly at your window, a peculiar weather event, a chance meeting, or repeating numbers and words, this journal will help you track and record the myriad ways in which the Universe has your back as it sends crucial, life-altering messages your way.

When you're aiming to make a decision, want to clarify your intentions, restore your sense of purpose, or simply feel the Universe's warm embrace, *Signs from the Universe* will help you navigate your way to the bright, gleaming future that awaits you.

LANGUAGES
of the
UNIVERSE

SIGNS AND SYMBOLS:

A sight that commands your attention—as if the Universe is winking at you or flagging you down. Signs and symbols inspire a search for meaning. Their energy gives you pause.

- Animals
- Colors
- Cosmic (a new moon, a shooting star, a constellation, etc.)
- Numbers (repeating or showing up again and again)
- Objects (lost, found, or revealed)
- Sounds (bells chiming, music, hearing your name called)
- Spirits (feeling the presence of, or seeing angels, ghosts, etc.)
- Weather events (a rainbow, a sudden downpour, lightning, etc.)

SYNCHRONICITIES:

The unexpected echo of your inner world in the external world. Synchronicities can lead you in a bold direction, answer a nagging question, or confirm something you already knew.

- Hearing a song that reflects your thoughts or emotions
- Seeing something or someone you've been thinking about
- An event or sighting that answers a question you've been asking yourself

DREAMS:

Cinematic sleep stories written and produced by the Universe itself. Dreams are the whispered truths your subconscious aims to relay to your consciousness.

- Babies and birth
- Being chased
- Being naked
- Death and dying
- Falling
- Flying
- Hidden rooms
- Childhood scenes
- Sexual scenarios
- Tests and school scenarios

GUT FEELINGS:

The secrets of the Universe stirring inside of you. A gut feeling is telling you what your mind is too stubborn to accept. When you trust your instincts and accept these truths, you have more power to manifest your best life.

- An inexplicable pull toward or away from something
- Déjà vu

ALL *the* VISIBLE UNIVERSE *is* NOTHING BUT *a* SHOP *of* IMAGES *and* SIGNS.

—CHARLES BAUDELAIRE

DATE:

TODAY, THE UNIVERSE COMMUNICATED THROUGH:

SIGNS AND SYMBOLS

DREAMS

SYNCHRONICITIES

GUT FEELINGS

WHAT IT MEANS TO ME:

WHAT IT INSPIRES ME TO DO:

DATE:

TODAY, THE UNIVERSE COMMUNICATED THROUGH:

SIGNS AND SYMBOLS

DREAMS

SYNCHRONICITIES

GUT FEELINGS

WHAT IT MEANS TO ME:

WHAT IT INSPIRES ME TO DO:

Angel Numbers Decoded

Repeating numbers signify that you are in the hands of a greater force. To some, that force is the Universe; to others, an angel or a god. Whatever it is to you, use the chart below to decode any angel numbers that make an appearance in your life.

111
The Universe is listening, so trust your intuition and tell it what you want. Love is all around you.

222
Look for balance and nurture your current relationships. All is well.

333
Take stock of the gifts and blessings you already have. Trust yourself.

444
The Universe wants you to work hard and stay grounded. Finish what you have started.

555
Big changes are on the way. Embrace the coming transformation.

666
Work on healing and fixing bad habits. Look deep into the Universe and reflect.

777
Luck is on the rise. Dig deep into your spirituality. The Universe has your back.

888
Abundance and wealth await you.

999
A cycle is ending. A new era is beginning. Let go of what doesn't serve you well in your life.

DATE:

TODAY, THE UNIVERSE COMMUNICATED THROUGH:

SIGNS AND SYMBOLS

DREAMS

SYNCHRONICITIES

GUT FEELINGS

WHAT IT MEANS TO ME:

WHAT IT INSPIRES ME TO DO:

DATE:

TODAY, THE UNIVERSE COMMUNICATED THROUGH:

SIGNS AND SYMBOLS

DREAMS

SYNCHRONICITIES

GUT FEELINGS

WHAT IT MEANS TO ME:

WHAT IT INSPIRES ME TO DO:

TODAY, THE UNIVERSE COMMUNICATED THROUGH:

SIGNS AND SYMBOLS

DREAMS

SYNCHRONICITIES

GUT FEELINGS

WHAT IT MEANS TO ME:

WHAT IT INSPIRES ME TO DO:

Animal Symbols Decoded

WOLF
instincts, social ties

HAWK
clear vision, new perspective

OWL
wisdom, seeing more

FOX
agility, clarity, intelligence

BEAR
strength and confidence

BUTTERFLY
rebirth, transformation, hope

IN EVERY MOMENT,
THE UNIVERSE IS
WHISPERING TO YOU.
YOU'RE CONSTANTLY
SURROUNDED BY

*signs, coincidences,
and synchronicities,*

ALL AIMED AT PROPELLING
YOU IN THE DIRECTION
OF YOUR DESTINY.

—Denise Linn

Use the Law of Attraction

The law of attraction is the guiding belief that like attracts like. That positive thinking is a form of energy and will yield positive results. In the same way, negative thoughts and energy can spark negative outcomes in your life. While you are paying attention to signs from the Universe, be mindful of interpreting them in the most positive way possible. If you are confronting the end of a relationship or job, take care to frame it as the start of something new.

GET YOUR POSITIVE ENERGY FLOWING.
WRITE FIVE POSITIVE THOUGHTS OR INTENTIONS BELOW:

1.

_____

2.

_____

3.

_____

4.

_____

5.

_____

DATE:

TODAY, THE UNIVERSE COMMUNICATED THROUGH:

SIGNS AND SYMBOLS

DREAMS

SYNCHRONICITIES

GUT FEELINGS

WHAT IT MEANS TO ME:

WHAT IT INSPIRES ME TO DO:

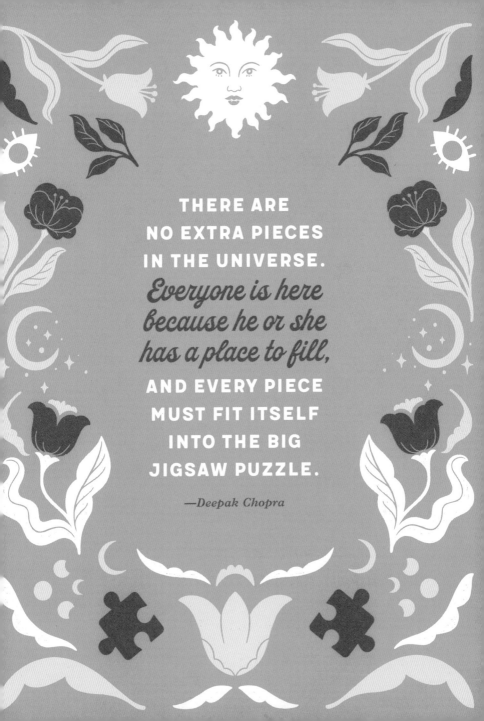

THERE ARE
NO EXTRA PIECES
IN THE UNIVERSE.
*Everyone is here
because he or she
has a place to fill,*
AND EVERY PIECE
MUST FIT ITSELF
INTO THE BIG
JIGSAW PUZZLE.

—Deepak Chopra

TODAY, THE UNIVERSE COMMUNICATED THROUGH:

SIGNS AND SYMBOLS

DREAMS

SYNCHRONICITIES

GUT FEELINGS

WHAT IT MEANS TO ME:

WHAT IT INSPIRES ME TO DO:

TODAY, THE UNIVERSE COMMUNICATED THROUGH:

SIGNS AND SYMBOLS

DREAMS

SYNCHRONICITIES

GUT FEELINGS

WHAT IT MEANS TO ME:

WHAT IT INSPIRES ME TO DO:

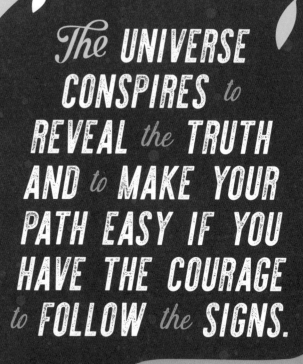

The UNIVERSE
CONSPIRES *to*
REVEAL *the* TRUTH
AND *to* MAKE YOUR
PATH EASY IF YOU
HAVE THE COURAGE
to FOLLOW *the* SIGNS.

—LISA UNGER

DATE:

TODAY, THE UNIVERSE COMMUNICATED THROUGH:

SIGNS AND SYMBOLS

DREAMS

SYNCHRONICITIES

GUT FEELINGS

WHAT IT MEANS TO ME:

WHAT IT INSPIRES ME TO DO:

DATE:

TODAY, THE UNIVERSE COMMUNICATED THROUGH:

SIGNS AND SYMBOLS

DREAMS

SYNCHRONICITIES

GUT FEELINGS

WHAT IT MEANS TO ME:

WHAT IT INSPIRES ME TO DO:

EVERY SINGLE ONE of US is a UNIQUE VIBRATION in a BEAUTIFUL SYMPHONY of INFINITE CREATION.

—GORDANA BIERNAT

What Colors Are Telling You

BLUE
be honest, practice
forgiveness, and communicate

PURPLE
listen to your intuition, express
your sensual and spiritual sides

ORANGE
get creative, stay
positive, look for joy

RED
use your power, follow
your passion

WHITE
get rid of what's not working,
declutter your mind and home

YELLOW
use your energy, gather your
willpower, shine like the sun

GREEN
take time to heal, find
ways to grow

BLACK
protect yourself, reflect
on life's mysteries

GOLD
Be open to prosperity
and enlightenment

PINK
explore your femininity,
look for romance

TODAY, THE UNIVERSE COMMUNICATED THROUGH:

SIGNS AND SYMBOLS

DREAMS

SYNCHRONICITIES

GUT FEELINGS

WHAT IT MEANS TO ME:

WHAT IT INSPIRES ME TO DO:

DATE:

TODAY, THE UNIVERSE COMMUNICATED THROUGH:

SIGNS AND SYMBOLS

DREAMS

SYNCHRONICITIES

GUT FEELINGS

WHAT IT MEANS TO ME:

WHAT IT INSPIRES ME TO DO:

DATE:

TODAY, THE UNIVERSE COMMUNICATED THROUGH:

SIGNS AND SYMBOLS

DREAMS

SYNCHRONICITIES

GUT FEELINGS

WHAT IT MEANS TO ME:

WHAT IT INSPIRES ME TO DO:

All you have to do is to pay attention; LESSONS ALWAYS ARRIVE WHEN YOU ARE READY, AND IF YOU CAN READ THE SIGNS, *you will learn everything you need* TO KNOW IN ORDER TO TAKE THE NEXT STEP.

—Paulo Coelho

TODAY, THE UNIVERSE COMMUNICATED THROUGH:

SIGNS AND SYMBOLS

DREAMS

SYNCHRONICITIES

GUT FEELINGS

WHAT IT MEANS TO ME:

WHAT IT INSPIRES ME TO DO:

DATE:

TODAY, THE UNIVERSE COMMUNICATED THROUGH:

SIGNS AND SYMBOLS

DREAMS

SYNCHRONICITIES

GUT FEELINGS

WHAT IT MEANS TO ME:

WHAT IT INSPIRES ME TO DO:

Guidance from the Night Sky

SHOOTING STARS

enlightenment, guidance, luck

ECLIPSE

change, growth, unexpected opportunities

METEOR SHOWER

spiritual awakening, emotions or fears coming to the surface

NEW MOON

second chances, hope, faith, beginnings

FULL MOON

gratitude, celebration, heightened emotions

TODAY, THE UNIVERSE COMMUNICATED THROUGH:

SIGNS AND SYMBOLS

DREAMS

SYNCHRONICITIES

GUT FEELINGS

WHAT IT MEANS TO ME:

WHAT IT INSPIRES ME TO DO:

TODAY, THE UNIVERSE COMMUNICATED THROUGH:

SIGNS AND SYMBOLS

DREAMS

SYNCHRONICITIES

GUT FEELINGS

WHAT IT MEANS TO ME:

WHAT IT INSPIRES ME TO DO:

DATE:

TODAY, THE UNIVERSE COMMUNICATED THROUGH:

SIGNS AND SYMBOLS

DREAMS

SYNCHRONICITIES

GUT FEELINGS

WHAT IT MEANS TO ME:

WHAT IT INSPIRES ME TO DO:

The UNIVERSE'S IMAGINATION ALWAYS REMAINS WIDER THAN OUR HUMAN IMAGINATIONS.

—Julie J. Morley

LOOK AT THE SKY.
We are not alone.
THE WHOLE UNIVERSE
IS FRIENDLY TO US AND
CONSPIRES ONLY TO
GIVE THE BEST TO THOSE
WHO DREAM AND WORK.

—*A. P. J. Abdul Kalam*

TODAY, THE UNIVERSE COMMUNICATED THROUGH:

SIGNS AND SYMBOLS

DREAMS

SYNCHRONICITIES

GUT FEELINGS

WHAT IT MEANS TO ME:

WHAT IT INSPIRES ME TO DO:

DATE:

TODAY, THE UNIVERSE COMMUNICATED THROUGH:

SIGNS AND SYMBOLS

DREAMS

SYNCHRONICITIES

GUT FEELINGS

WHAT IT MEANS TO ME:

WHAT IT INSPIRES ME TO DO:

The Wisdom of Weather

Weather is one way for the Universe to send us messages. Whether it's a harbinger of something to come or a mirror held up to our emotional world, reading the sky and noticing the natural world around us can help guide us on our journey.

WIND
upcoming change

FOG
uncertainty, feeling lost

RAIN
fertility, purification, washing away negativity

STORM
chaos, trauma, repressed anger

RAINBOW
renewal, positivity, hope

SNOW
purity, innocence

LIGHTNING
power, clarity, illumination

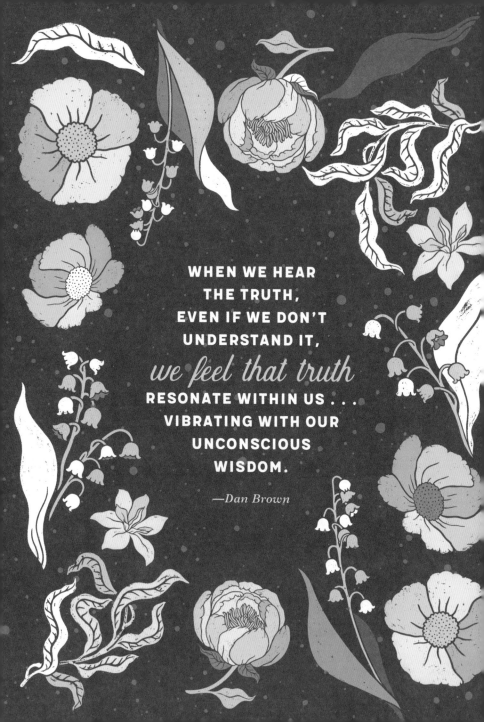

WHEN WE HEAR
THE TRUTH,
EVEN IF WE DON'T
UNDERSTAND IT,
we feel that truth
RESONATE WITHIN US . . .
VIBRATING WITH OUR
UNCONSCIOUS
WISDOM.

—*Dan Brown*

TODAY, THE UNIVERSE COMMUNICATED THROUGH:

SIGNS AND SYMBOLS

DREAMS

SYNCHRONICITIES

GUT FEELINGS

WHAT IT MEANS TO ME:

WHAT IT INSPIRES ME TO DO:

DATE:

TODAY, THE UNIVERSE COMMUNICATED THROUGH:

SIGNS AND SYMBOLS

DREAMS

SYNCHRONICITIES

GUT FEELINGS

WHAT IT MEANS TO ME:

WHAT IT INSPIRES ME TO DO:

DATE:

TODAY, THE UNIVERSE COMMUNICATED THROUGH:

SIGNS AND SYMBOLS

DREAMS

SYNCHRONICITIES

GUT FEELINGS

WHAT IT MEANS TO ME:

WHAT IT INSPIRES ME TO DO:

DATE:

TODAY, THE UNIVERSE COMMUNICATED THROUGH:

SIGNS AND SYMBOLS

DREAMS

SYNCHRONICITIES

GUT FEELINGS

WHAT IT MEANS TO ME:

WHAT IT INSPIRES ME TO DO:

ALL THE POWERS IN THE
Universe are already ours.
**IT IS WE WHO HAVE PUT OUR
HANDS BEFORE OUR EYES
AND CRY THAT IT IS DARK.**

—Swami Vivekananda

Spirits and Ghosts

Connecting to the spirit world and those who have passed can open our hearts and minds to other dimensions of the vast Universe. Any of these signs can indicate the presence of spirit guides.

Flashing lights or
an electric surge

A pet or animal
acting strangely

Smelling a perfume or cologne
that reminds you of the deceased

Sensing a touch
or a presence

Things falling or
moving unexpectedly

Chills or goosebumps

Hearing a voice or a whisper

A sudden change
in temperature

DATE:

TODAY, THE UNIVERSE COMMUNICATED THROUGH:

SIGNS AND SYMBOLS

DREAMS

SYNCHRONICITIES

GUT FEELINGS

WHAT IT MEANS TO ME:

WHAT IT INSPIRES ME TO DO:

TODAY, THE UNIVERSE COMMUNICATED THROUGH:

SIGNS AND SYMBOLS

DREAMS

SYNCHRONICITIES

GUT FEELINGS

WHAT IT MEANS TO ME:

WHAT IT INSPIRES ME TO DO:

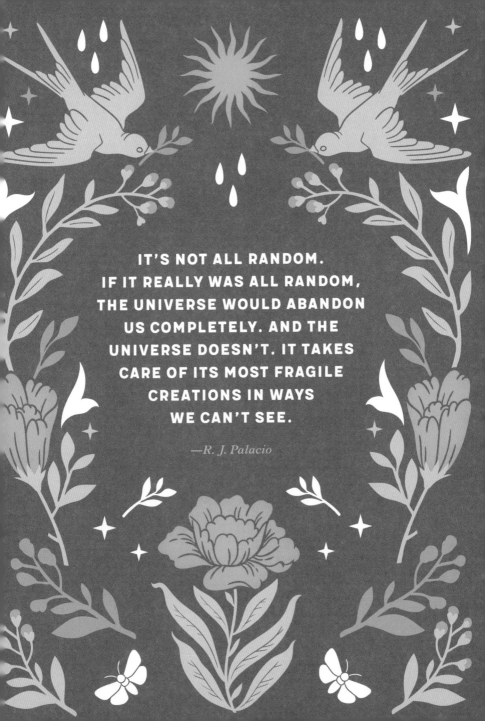

IT'S NOT ALL RANDOM.
IF IT REALLY WAS ALL RANDOM,
THE UNIVERSE WOULD ABANDON
US COMPLETELY. AND THE
UNIVERSE DOESN'T. IT TAKES
CARE OF ITS MOST FRAGILE
CREATIONS IN WAYS
WE CAN'T SEE.

—*R. J. Palacio*

DATE:

TODAY, THE UNIVERSE COMMUNICATED THROUGH:

SIGNS AND SYMBOLS

DREAMS

SYNCHRONICITIES

GUT FEELINGS

WHAT IT MEANS TO ME:

WHAT IT INSPIRES ME TO DO:

DATE:

TODAY, THE UNIVERSE COMMUNICATED THROUGH:

SIGNS AND SYMBOLS

DREAMS

SYNCHRONICITIES

GUT FEELINGS

WHAT IT MEANS TO ME:

WHAT IT INSPIRES ME TO DO:

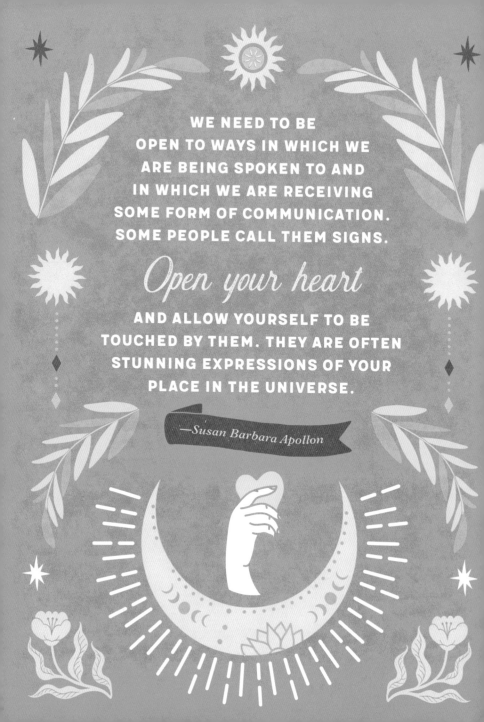

WE NEED TO BE
OPEN TO WAYS IN WHICH WE
ARE BEING SPOKEN TO AND
IN WHICH WE ARE RECEIVING
SOME FORM OF COMMUNICATION.
SOME PEOPLE CALL THEM SIGNS.

Open your heart

AND ALLOW YOURSELF TO BE
TOUCHED BY THEM. THEY ARE OFTEN
STUNNING EXPRESSIONS OF YOUR
PLACE IN THE UNIVERSE.

—Susan Barbara Apollon

TODAY, THE UNIVERSE COMMUNICATED THROUGH:

SIGNS AND SYMBOLS

DREAMS

SYNCHRONICITIES

GUT FEELINGS

WHAT IT MEANS TO ME:

WHAT IT INSPIRES ME TO DO:

DATE:

TODAY, THE UNIVERSE COMMUNICATED THROUGH:

SIGNS AND SYMBOLS

DREAMS

SYNCHRONICITIES

GUT FEELINGS

WHAT IT MEANS TO ME:

WHAT IT INSPIRES ME TO DO:

Meaningful Number Sequences

Pay attention to sequences of numbers that may appear around you to convey a special meaning.

birth dates

street addresses

flight numbers

lottery numbers

parking space numbers

license plate numbers

telephone numbers

numbers that add up
to an important number

your INNER VOICE *is* YOUR SIGNBOARD, FOLLOW IT.

—*Anamika Mishra*

TODAY, THE UNIVERSE COMMUNICATED THROUGH:

SIGNS AND SYMBOLS

DREAMS

SYNCHRONICITIES

GUT FEELINGS

WHAT IT MEANS TO ME:

WHAT IT INSPIRES ME TO DO:

TODAY, THE UNIVERSE COMMUNICATED THROUGH:

SIGNS AND SYMBOLS

DREAMS

SYNCHRONICITIES

GUT FEELINGS

WHAT IT MEANS TO ME:

WHAT IT INSPIRES ME TO DO:

Birds as Symbols

Birds represent different forces in our lives.
Consider them the Universe's feathered
messengers; its own system of airmail.

CRANE
peace, good fortune

CARDINAL
balance, mystery

EAGLE
strength, renewal

BLUEBIRD
joy, truth

SPARROW
hard work, creativity

CROW
change, adaption

HUMMINGBIRD
happiness, healing

EVERYTHING YOU'LL
EVER NEED TO
KNOW IS WITHIN YOU;
the secrets of the Universe
ARE IMPRINTED ON THE
CELLS OF YOUR BODY.

—*Dan Millman*

TODAY, THE UNIVERSE COMMUNICATED THROUGH:

SIGNS AND SYMBOLS

DREAMS

SYNCHRONICITIES

GUT FEELINGS

WHAT IT MEANS TO ME:

WHAT IT INSPIRES ME TO DO:

TODAY, THE UNIVERSE COMMUNICATED THROUGH:

SIGNS AND SYMBOLS

DREAMS

SYNCHRONICITIES

GUT FEELINGS

WHAT IT MEANS TO ME:

WHAT IT INSPIRES ME TO DO:

DATE:

TODAY, THE UNIVERSE COMMUNICATED THROUGH:

SIGNS AND SYMBOLS

DREAMS

SYNCHRONICITIES

GUT FEELINGS

WHAT IT MEANS TO ME:

WHAT IT INSPIRES ME TO DO:

TODAY, THE UNIVERSE COMMUNICATED THROUGH:

SIGNS AND SYMBOLS

DREAMS

SYNCHRONICITIES

GUT FEELINGS

WHAT IT MEANS TO ME:

WHAT IT INSPIRES ME TO DO:

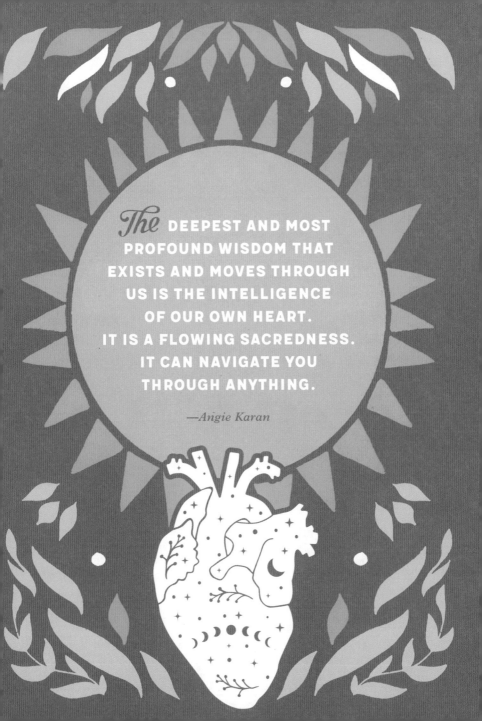

The DEEPEST AND MOST
PROFOUND WISDOM THAT
EXISTS AND MOVES THROUGH
US IS THE INTELLIGENCE
OF OUR OWN HEART.
IT IS A FLOWING SACREDNESS.
IT CAN NAVIGATE YOU
THROUGH ANYTHING.

—*Angie Karan*

Tune in and Listen

The Universe communicates in meaningful sounds
sent at opportune times. Whether it comes to you
as music or chimes or words carried on the wind,
keep your ears open to the many ways in which the
Universe whispers its guiding truths.

CHIRPING BIRDS

a call for serenity

CROAKING FROG

abundance and fertility

BELLS

call to action, communication
from spirits or angels

CHIMES

good luck, protection from evil

RINGING IN YOUR LEFT EAR

warning, call to action,
something is amiss

RINGING IN YOUR RIGHT EAR

comfort, companionship,
reassurance

The
VISIBLE
WORLD IS A
DAILY MIRACLE,
FOR THOSE
WHO HAVE
EYES AND EARS.

—EDITH WHARTON

DATE:

TODAY, THE UNIVERSE COMMUNICATED THROUGH:

SIGNS AND SYMBOLS

DREAMS

SYNCHRONICITIES

GUT FEELINGS

WHAT IT MEANS TO ME:

WHAT IT INSPIRES ME TO DO:

TODAY, THE UNIVERSE COMMUNICATED THROUGH:

SIGNS AND SYMBOLS

DREAMS

SYNCHRONICITIES

GUT FEELINGS

WHAT IT MEANS TO ME:

WHAT IT INSPIRES ME TO DO:

DATE:

TODAY, THE UNIVERSE COMMUNICATED THROUGH:

SIGNS AND SYMBOLS

DREAMS

SYNCHRONICITIES

GUT FEELINGS·

WHAT IT MEANS TO ME:

WHAT IT INSPIRES ME TO DO:

TODAY, THE UNIVERSE COMMUNICATED THROUGH:

SIGNS AND SYMBOLS

DREAMS

SYNCHRONICITIES

GUT FEELINGS

WHAT IT MEANS TO ME:

WHAT IT INSPIRES ME TO DO:

WE ARE THE COSMOS MADE CONSCIOUS AND LIFE IS THE MEANS BY WHICH THE UNIVERSE UNDERSTANDS ITSELF.

—Brian Cox

Objects Lost and Found

Lost items can encourage you to reflect on how much
they matter to you, whereas found objects can renew your
appreciation for them. Pay attention to the little phenomena.

LOST KEYS
know where you're headed

RECOVERED OBJECT
revisit the past,
practice gratitude

LOST MONEY
consider what you value most

BROKEN OBJECT
letting go of the past
or a connection

LOST RING
reflect on your relationship(s)

NEWFOUND OBJECT
discovery, inspiration

DATE:

TODAY, THE UNIVERSE COMMUNICATED THROUGH:

SIGNS AND SYMBOLS

DREAMS

SYNCHRONICITIES

GUT FEELINGS

WHAT IT MEANS TO ME:

WHAT IT INSPIRES ME TO DO:

DATE:

TODAY, THE UNIVERSE COMMUNICATED THROUGH:

SIGNS AND SYMBOLS

DREAMS

SYNCHRONICITIES

GUT FEELINGS

WHAT IT MEANS TO ME:

WHAT IT INSPIRES ME TO DO:

The

PHYSICAL UNIVERSE AND *its* BUZZING MACHINERY, *its* FANTASTICAL SCENERY.

—*Laura Kasischke*

TODAY, THE UNIVERSE COMMUNICATED THROUGH:

SIGNS AND SYMBOLS

DREAMS

SYNCHRONICITIES

GUT FEELINGS

WHAT IT MEANS TO ME:

WHAT IT INSPIRES ME TO DO:

TODAY, THE UNIVERSE COMMUNICATED THROUGH:

SIGNS AND SYMBOLS

DREAMS

SYNCHRONICITIES

GUT FEELINGS

WHAT IT MEANS TO ME:

WHAT IT INSPIRES ME TO DO:

The GREATEST MINDS HAVE ALWAYS UNDERSTOOD THAT THEY CAN LISTEN TO THE UNIVERSE.

—Steve Madison

DATE:

TODAY, THE UNIVERSE COMMUNICATED THROUGH:

SIGNS AND SYMBOLS

DREAMS

SYNCHRONICITIES

GUT FEELINGS

WHAT IT MEANS TO ME:

WHAT IT INSPIRES ME TO DO:

TODAY, THE UNIVERSE COMMUNICATED THROUGH:

SIGNS AND SYMBOLS

DREAMS

SYNCHRONICITIES

GUT FEELINGS

WHAT IT MEANS TO ME:

WHAT IT INSPIRES ME TO DO:

How to Know if it's a Sign

If you're not sure if something is a sign from the Universe, trust your instincts. Here are some clues that the Universe is speaking to you.

You're waiting for an answer
or you've asked for guidance

The sign is surprising,
out of place, or unlikely

It gives you chills
or a physical reaction

It causes you to feel
a surge of emotion

There's something
familiar about the sign

DATE:

TODAY, THE UNIVERSE COMMUNICATED THROUGH:

SIGNS AND SYMBOLS

DREAMS

SYNCHRONICITIES

GUT FEELINGS

WHAT IT MEANS TO ME:

WHAT IT INSPIRES ME TO DO:

TODAY, THE UNIVERSE COMMUNICATED THROUGH:

SIGNS AND SYMBOLS

DREAMS

SYNCHRONICITIES

GUT FEELINGS

WHAT IT MEANS TO ME:

WHAT IT INSPIRES ME TO DO:

I HAD THE EPIPHANY THAT
laughter was light,
AND LIGHT WAS LAUGHTER,
AND THAT THIS WAS THE
SECRET OF THE UNIVERSE.

—*Donna Tartt*

TODAY, THE UNIVERSE COMMUNICATED THROUGH:

SIGNS AND SYMBOLS

DREAMS

SYNCHRONICITIES

GUT FEELINGS

WHAT IT MEANS TO ME:

WHAT IT INSPIRES ME TO DO:

DATE:

TODAY, THE UNIVERSE COMMUNICATED THROUGH:

SIGNS AND SYMBOLS

DREAMS

SYNCHRONICITIES

GUT FEELINGS

WHAT IT MEANS TO ME:

WHAT IT INSPIRES ME TO DO:

THINK HAPPY AND HAPPINESS WILL COME TO YOU. THINK NEGATIVELY AND NEGATIVITY WILL COME TO YOU.

What we put out into the Universe, we get back like an echo.

−ABRAHAM HICKS

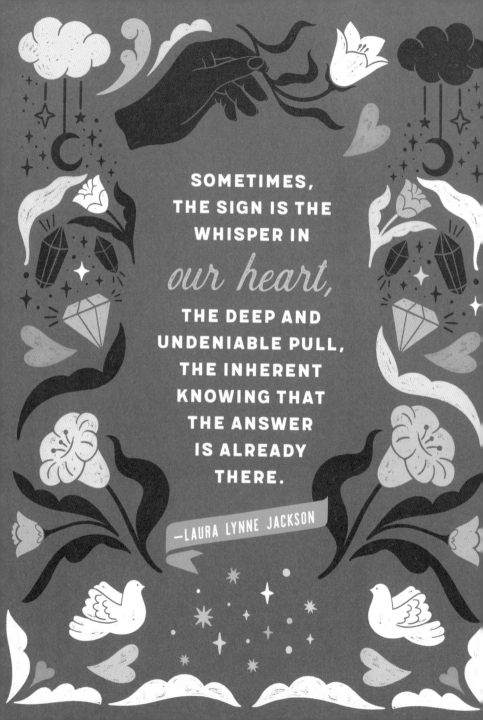

SOMETIMES,
THE SIGN IS THE
WHISPER IN
our heart,
THE DEEP AND
UNDENIABLE PULL,
THE INHERENT
KNOWING THAT
THE ANSWER
IS ALREADY
THERE.

—LAURA LYNNE JACKSON

TODAY, THE UNIVERSE COMMUNICATED THROUGH:

SIGNS AND SYMBOLS

DREAMS

SYNCHRONICITIES

GUT FEELINGS

WHAT IT MEANS TO ME:

WHAT IT INSPIRES ME TO DO:

DATE:

TODAY, THE UNIVERSE COMMUNICATED THROUGH:

SIGNS AND SYMBOLS

DREAMS

SYNCHRONICITIES

GUT FEELINGS

WHAT IT MEANS TO ME:

WHAT IT INSPIRES ME TO DO:

DATE:

TODAY, THE UNIVERSE COMMUNICATED THROUGH:

SIGNS AND SYMBOLS

DREAMS

SYNCHRONICITIES

GUT FEELINGS

WHAT IT MEANS TO ME:

WHAT IT INSPIRES ME TO DO:

TODAY, THE UNIVERSE COMMUNICATED THROUGH:

SIGNS AND SYMBOLS

DREAMS

SYNCHRONICITIES

GUT FEELINGS

WHAT IT MEANS TO ME:

WHAT IT INSPIRES ME TO DO:

OUR BIOLOGICAL
RHYTHMS ARE THE
SYMPHONY OF THE COSMOS,
MUSIC EMBEDDED DEEP
WITHIN US TO WHICH

we dance,

EVEN WHEN WE
CAN'T NAME THE TUNE.

—*Deepak Chopra*

There comes a
time when all the
cosmic tumblers have
clicked into place and the
Universe opens itself up for
a few seconds to show you
what is possible.

—*Ray Kinsella*, Field of Dreams

DATE:

TODAY, THE UNIVERSE COMMUNICATED THROUGH:

SIGNS AND SYMBOLS

DREAMS

SYNCHRONICITIES

GUT FEELINGS

WHAT IT MEANS TO ME:

WHAT IT INSPIRES ME TO DO:

TODAY, THE UNIVERSE COMMUNICATED THROUGH:

SIGNS AND SYMBOLS

DREAMS

SYNCHRONICITIES

GUT FEELINGS

WHAT IT MEANS TO ME:

WHAT IT INSPIRES ME TO DO:

Synchronicities Abound

Meaningful coincidences, also called synchronicities, are the
Universe's way of flagging you down to get your attention.
Watch for these uncanny occurrences in your daily life:

Hearing or seeing the
name of someone you
were just thinking about

A meaningful symbol (directional
sign, company logo, number,
word, etc.) that shows up in
your life more than once

Getting a lucky break
just when you need it

Seeing something you
just dreamed about

Hearing a song that
answers a question you've
been asking yourself

DATE:

TODAY, THE UNIVERSE COMMUNICATED THROUGH:

SIGNS AND SYMBOLS

DREAMS

SYNCHRONICITIES

GUT FEELINGS

WHAT IT MEANS TO ME:

WHAT IT INSPIRES ME TO DO:

DATE:

TODAY, THE UNIVERSE COMMUNICATED THROUGH:

SIGNS AND SYMBOLS

DREAMS

SYNCHRONICITIES

GUT FEELINGS

WHAT IT MEANS TO ME:

WHAT IT INSPIRES ME TO DO:

WHEN WE TRY TO PICK OUT ANYTHING BY ITSELF, WE FIND IT HITCHED TO EVERYTHING ELSE IN THE UNIVERSE.

—John Muir

DATE:

TODAY, THE UNIVERSE COMMUNICATED THROUGH:

SIGNS AND SYMBOLS

DREAMS

SYNCHRONICITIES

GUT FEELINGS

WHAT IT MEANS TO ME:

WHAT IT INSPIRES ME TO DO:

The Power of Dreams

To gain a deeper understanding of yourself and gather all the wisdom of the Universe, dive wholeheartedly into the mystery and wonder of your dreams.

 IN THE DEPTHS OF SLEEP, YOU BECOME MORE RECEPTIVE TO MESSAGES FROM OTHER WORLDS.

Your mind is permitted to roam freely in search of answers to your deepest questions.

NOT EVERY DREAM IS MEANINGFUL OR POSSIBLE TO DECODE.

The most powerful and important dreams are the ones that stay with you even after you wake up. Write them down (along with the feelings they inspired) and, without forcing answers, sift through them for valuable truths and messages.

EVERYONE HAS THEIR OWN DREAM VOCABULARY; A PERSONAL CODE OF SYMBOLS THAT ARE UNIQUE TO YOU.

As you become more familiar with your own dreamscapes and learn to recognize the emblems that reappear most often in them, you'll feel more confident translating their meaning.

DATE:

TODAY, THE UNIVERSE COMMUNICATED THROUGH:

SIGNS AND SYMBOLS

DREAMS

SYNCHRONICITIES

GUT FEELINGS

WHAT IT MEANS TO ME:

WHAT IT INSPIRES ME TO DO:

Dream Symbols

While we should always trust our instincts when interpreting our own dreams, here are some of the most common dream signposts. Use the questions here to guide your understanding and discover what the symbol means to you.

ANIMALS

How would you describe your connection to nature?

....

FALLING

What might you need to let go of?

What makes you feel like you're losing control or failing?

....

BABIES AND BIRTH

What is new in your life?

What makes you feel loved?
How might you be feeling vulnerable?

....

BEING CHASED

What are you deeply afraid of?
Why might it be hard to admit?

DEATH AND DYING

**What change are you
coping with in your life?**

....

FOOD

What knowledge are you seeking?

....

NUDITY

What are your deepest desires?

What is making you feel vulnerable?

....

TEETH FALLING OUT

**How do you feel about your
personal appearance?**

How do you feel about aging?

a DREAM NOT INTERPRETED *is* LIKE *a* LETTER NOT READ.

—*The Talmud, Berachot 55a*

DATE:

TODAY, THE UNIVERSE COMMUNICATED THROUGH:

SIGNS AND SYMBOLS

DREAMS

SYNCHRONICITIES

GUT FEELINGS

WHAT IT MEANS TO ME:

WHAT IT INSPIRES ME TO DO:

TODAY, THE UNIVERSE COMMUNICATED THROUGH:

SIGNS AND SYMBOLS

DREAMS

SYNCHRONICITIES

GUT FEELINGS

WHAT IT MEANS TO ME:

WHAT IT INSPIRES ME TO DO:

Dream Incubation

Dreams create a magical and powerful space where the wall between the physical and spiritual worlds disappears. Dream incubation is the practice of allowing your subconscious to prop open the door of your waking mind and let the Universe fill it with answers.

BEFORE YOU GO TO SLEEP AT NIGHT, WRITE A QUESTION TO THE UNIVERSE, OR DRAW A SYMBOL THAT KEEPS SHOWING UP IN YOUR LIFE.

Place it under your pillow. When you wake up, reflect on your dreams and consider how they might be offering you guidance.

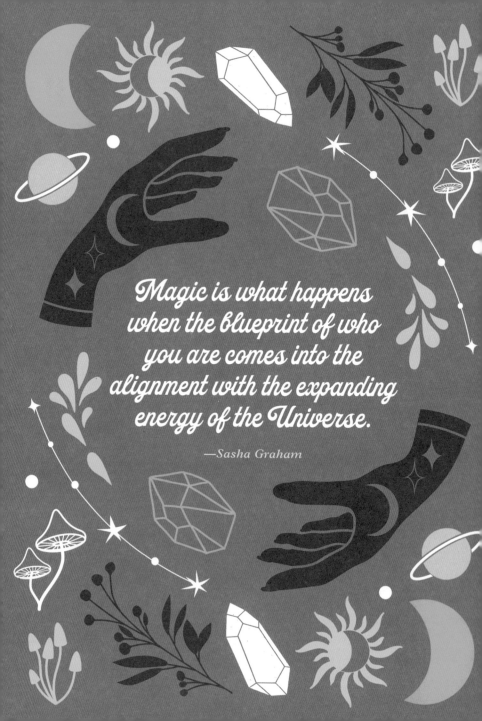

Magic is what happens when the blueprint of who you are comes into the alignment with the expanding energy of the Universe.

—*Sasha Graham*

DATE:

TODAY, THE UNIVERSE COMMUNICATED THROUGH:

SIGNS AND SYMBOLS

DREAMS

SYNCHRONICITIES

GUT FEELINGS

WHAT IT MEANS TO ME:

WHAT IT INSPIRES ME TO DO:

TODAY, THE UNIVERSE COMMUNICATED THROUGH:

SIGNS AND SYMBOLS

DREAMS

SYNCHRONICITIES

GUT FEELINGS

WHAT IT MEANS TO ME:

WHAT IT INSPIRES ME TO DO:

YOU & I ARE
ALL AS MUCH
CONTINUOUS WITH
THE PHYSICAL
UNIVERSE AS A WAVE
IS CONTINUOUS
WITH THE OCEAN.

—*Alan Watts*

DATE:

TODAY, THE UNIVERSE COMMUNICATED THROUGH:

SIGNS AND SYMBOLS

DREAMS

SYNCHRONICITIES

GUT FEELINGS

WHAT IT MEANS TO ME:

WHAT IT INSPIRES ME TO DO:

DATE:

TODAY, THE UNIVERSE COMMUNICATED THROUGH:

SIGNS AND SYMBOLS

DREAMS

SYNCHRONICITIES

GUT FEELINGS

WHAT IT MEANS TO ME:

WHAT IT INSPIRES ME TO DO:

The truth of
the stars
reflects
through
all of us.

—*Jordan G. Kobos*

TODAY, THE UNIVERSE COMMUNICATED THROUGH:

SIGNS AND SYMBOLS

DREAMS

SYNCHRONICITIES

GUT FEELINGS

WHAT IT MEANS TO ME:

WHAT IT INSPIRES ME TO DO:

TODAY, THE UNIVERSE COMMUNICATED THROUGH:

SIGNS AND SYMBOLS

DREAMS

SYNCHRONICITIES

GUT FEELINGS

WHAT IT MEANS TO ME:

WHAT IT INSPIRES ME TO DO:

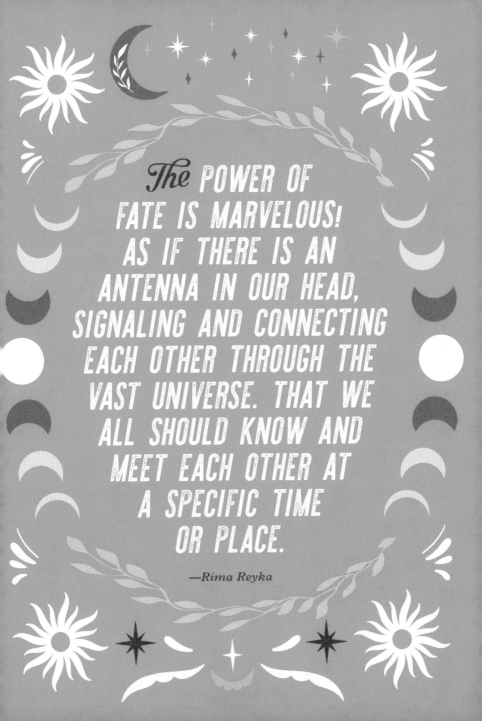

The POWER OF
FATE IS MARVELOUS!
AS IF THERE IS AN
ANTENNA IN OUR HEAD,
SIGNALING AND CONNECTING
EACH OTHER THROUGH THE
VAST UNIVERSE. THAT WE
ALL SHOULD KNOW AND
MEET EACH OTHER AT
A SPECIFIC TIME
OR PLACE.

—Rima Reyka

Setting Intentions

Communication with the Universe works both ways. Instead of simply waiting for the Universe to speak to you, sometimes you must send it a message.

 YOU ARE FULL OF POWERFUL ENERGY, SO HARNESS IT TO AFFECT POSITIVE CHANGE IN YOUR LIFE.

State your intention to the Universe, engaging your emotions as you do so. Write down what you want to happen or speak it out loud. Release that ripple of energy into the world and create waves of change.

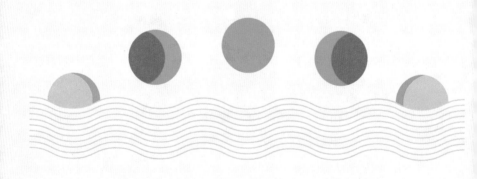

TODAY, THE UNIVERSE COMMUNICATED THROUGH:

SIGNS AND SYMBOLS

DREAMS

SYNCHRONICITIES

GUT FEELINGS

WHAT IT MEANS TO ME:

WHAT IT INSPIRES ME TO DO:

TODAY, THE UNIVERSE COMMUNICATED THROUGH:

SIGNS AND SYMBOLS

DREAMS

SYNCHRONICITIES

GUT FEELINGS

WHAT IT MEANS TO ME:

WHAT IT INSPIRES ME TO DO:

DATE:

TODAY, THE UNIVERSE COMMUNICATED THROUGH:

SIGNS AND SYMBOLS

DREAMS

SYNCHRONICITIES

GUT FEELINGS

WHAT IT MEANS TO ME:

WHAT IT INSPIRES ME TO DO:

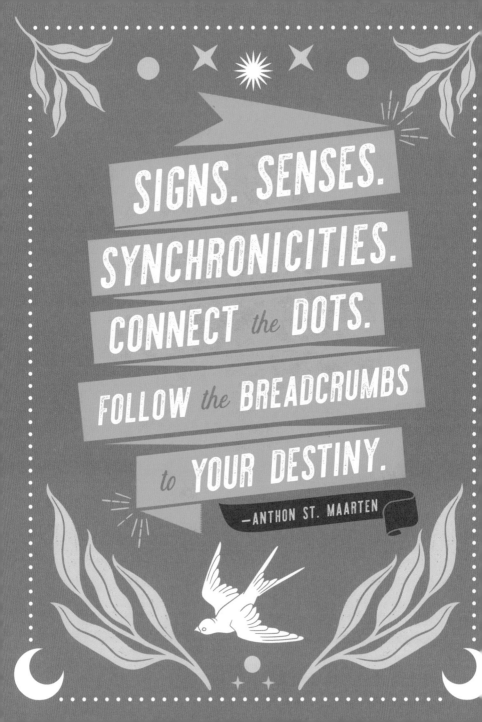

SIGNS. SENSES. SYNCHRONICITIES. CONNECT the DOTS. FOLLOW the BREADCRUMBS to YOUR DESTINY.

—ANTHON ST. MAARTEN